Anonymus

Returns of local taxation in Ireland 1893

Anonymus

Returns of local taxation in Ireland 1893

ISBN/EAN: 9783742811080

Manufactured in Europe, USA, Canada, Australia, Japa

Cover: Foto ©Suzi / pixelio.de

Manufactured and distributed by brebook publishing software
(www.brebook.com)

Anonymus

Returns of local taxation in Ireland 1893

LOCAL TAXATION (IRELAND) RETURNS.

RETURNS

-

LOCAL TAXATION IN IRELAND,

FOR THE

YEAR 1893.

COLLECTED AND COMPILED UNDER THE DIRECTION OF THE LOCAL GOVERNMENT BOARD
BY DESIRE OF

HIS EXCELLENCY THE LORD LIECTENANT OF IRELAND.

Presented to both Houses of Parliament by Command of Her Majesty.

DUBLIN:
PRINTED FOR HER MAJESTY'S STATIONERY OFFICE,
BY ALEXANDER THOM & CO. (LIMITED).

And to be purchased, either directly or through any Bookseller, from
Hodges, Figgis, and Co. (Limited), 104, Grafton-street, Dublin; or
Eyre and Spottiswoode, East Harding-street, Fleet-street, E.C.; or
John Menzies and Co., 12, Hanover-street, Edinburgh, and 90, West Nile-street, Glasgow.

1894.

TABLE OF CONTENTS.

APPENDIXES.

RETURNS of LOCAL TAXATION classified according to the objects to which TAXATION is applied.

INTRODUCTORY AND EXPLANATORY OBSERVATIONS.

I. TOTAL AMOUNT OF LOCAL TAXATION OF IRELAND.

THE local taxation of Ireland, making the deductions ascertained to be necessary on account of sums which appear twice in the receipts of local authorities consequent on the fact that contributions are sometimes made from the taxation of one local authority towards the expenditure of another, may be set down for the year 1893 at £3,697,940, being an increase of £107,710, or 3 per cent. on the amount in the previous year.

This sum is compared with the corresponding amounts in preceding years since 1866, in the following table :—

Year.	Local taxation of Ireland.	Increase.	Decrease.	Increase per cent.	Decrease per cent.
	£	£	£		
1866, . . .	2,535,230	—	—	—	—
1867, . . .	2,589,651	51,401	—	1·2	—
1868, . . .	2,712,104	172,423	—	7	—
1869, . . .	2,767,777	5,673	—	·1	—
1870, . . .	2,738,337	—	19,430	—	·7
1871, . . .	2,786,749	58,123	—	·1	—
1872, . . .	2,905,250	118,501	—	4·1	—
1873, . . .	2,981,539	76,070	—	2·6	—
1874, . . .	3,117,828	166,005	—	6·6	—
1875, . . .	3,163,945	45,517	—	1·5	—
1876, . . .	3,344,083	49,145	—	1·6	—
1877, . . .	3,101,513	—	78,960	—	8·4
1878, . . .	3,251,452	84,838	—	8·7	—
1879, . . .	3,368,133	116,591	—	3·6	—
1880, . . .	3,299,541	—	76,073	—	8·4
1881, . . .	3,391,480	85,838	—	3	—
1882, . . .	3,534,878	143,349	—	4·2	—
1883, . . .	3,774,316	245,436	—	5·9	—
1884, . . .	3,785,940	10,625	—	·4	—
1885, . . .	3,631,100	—	107,830	—	1·6
1886, . . .	3,492,672	—	198,446	—	8·6
1887, . . .	3,540,103	47,431	—	1·4	—
1888, . . .	3,675,473	84,349	—	1	—
1889, . . .	3,663,207	27,735	—	·6	—
1890, . . .	3,558,093	—	104,114	—	8·4
1891, . . .	3,503,519	—	54,574	—	1·6
1892, . . .	3,590,329	85,707	—	2·4	—
1893, . . .	3,697,940	107,710	—	5	—

As regards the amount of taxation given in the foregoing table for the year 1892, it will be observed from the introductory observations to the Returns for that year that at the time of their completion our local returns had not been received, and, as certain other returns of town taxation had been furnished before the accounts of those towns were audited, it has been found necessary to revise the town taxation for that year in so far as relates to the cases referred to.

The Grand Jury taxation for 1893 has also been revised to the extent of including in the total taxation of the year only the amount of Grand Jury Cess which had been collected instead of the amounts authorised to be levied, as had formerly been the practice. This revision was rendered necessary in order to obtain a correct comparison with the year 1892, inasmuch as the total taxation for that year given on the preceding page, viz.: £3,697,919, includes the amount of cess collected and applied towards the year's expenditure, as shown in a new table on pages 16 and 17, which has been prepared from the abstracts of County accounts furnished after audit by the Auditors of the Local Government Board.

Analysof taxation in totalled in 1893.	Increase, as compared with 1892.	Decrease, as compared with 1892.
	£	£
1. Grand Jury cess, ...	—	3,850
2. Fees of Clerks of the Peace, . .	39	—
3. Fees of Clerks of the Crown, . . .	95	—
4. Petty Sessions stamps and Crown fines, and dividends,	108	—
5. Dog Licence duty, and dividends, . .	853	—
6. Dublin Metropolitan Police taxes, . .	1,825	—
7. Court Leet presentments, ...	—	—
8. Harbour taxation (exclusive of receipts from Grand Jury cess, and from sale of investments), .	—	20,405
9. Inland navigation taxation, ...	1,217	—
10. Taxation under Town Authorities (exclusive of receipts from Dog Licence duty, Fines, Grand Jury cess, &c.),	67,853	—
11. Burial Board receipts other than from cess (exclusive of what is received by urban Boards),	—	629
12. Poor rate and other amounts of Boards of Guardians (exclusive of repayment of rates, and of the Burial Board receipts included in No. 11, .	74,796	—
13. Light dues, and fees under Merchant Shipping Act, .	352	—
Total increase, ...	147,134	—
Deduct decrease, ...	—	39,434
Net increase, as shown on preceding page, .	107,710	—

It will be seen from the foregoing analysis that compared with the previous year there was in 1893 a decrease of £3,850 in Grand Jury cess, and of £20,405 in Harbour taxation, while there was an increase of £67,953 in the taxation by town authorities, and of £74,796 in that by Boards of Guardians. In reference to the increase in the amount of the taxation by Boards of Guardians in 1893 as compared with 1892, it may be noted that the amount in the latter year, viz., £997,827, was lower than in any of the preceding years since 1878, and that the amount in 1893, viz., £1,072,123, was less than the average of the years from 1878 to 1893, inclusive.

The Grant in aid of local taxation provided by the Probate Duties (Scotland and Ireland) Act, 1888, amounted to £310,068 for the year ended the 31st of March, 1893, of which one-half was received by Boards of Guardians (as shown in Appendix XVII., page 44), and the other half by Road Authorities, viz., £85,568 by Grand Juries, and £19,505 by certain Town Authorities. The towns which participate in the Grant, and the sum received by each of them in respect of the year in question are shown in Table III. of the Appendix, page 43.

2. Grand Jury Cess.

One of the oldest and the largest of the local taxes in Ireland is the rate on real property called Grand Jury cess. It derives this name from the Authority chiefly engaged in authorizing its application. The origin of this tax, and the constitution of the bodies that administer it, are fully explained in former Reports.

The following is a classification of the gross amount of Grand Jury cess under the principal heads of the expenditure proposed:—

	£	Percentage of total
Roads and bridges,	721,488	51·28
Maintenance of lunatic asylums,	157,144	10·71
Miscellaneous,	225,040	15·34
Salaries of County officers,	102,375	6·98
Prison expenses,	18,117	1·3
In discharge of debt :—		
To Government,	275,326	
To others than Government,	6,440	
	51,768	3·97
Infirmaries, hospitals, &c.	20,578	1·45
Extra police,	27,344	1·86
Valuation,	4,840	·33
Erecting and repairs of Court and Sessions' houses,	7,644	·44
Police for weights and measures,	6,885	·4
Total,	£1,466,910	100

The re-presentments and other credits included in this total amounted to £212,584, and the deduction of this sum left a net amount of £1,254,226 to be levied in the year 1893.

The receipts of County Authorities in the year 1892, excluding the counties of the cities of Cork, Dublin, and Limerick which are not under Grand Jury management for fiscal purposes,* amounted to £1,403,721, and this is summarized as follows :—

	£	Percentage of total
Amount of Grand Jury cess collected,	1,212,701	86·68
From Imperial taxes,	125,168	8·9
From local rates or taxes,	25,385	1·82
From land,	7,150	·5
From other sources (including £5,907 received from Dog Licence Duty),	29,846	2·1
Total,	£1,403,721	100

3. Officers of Local Courts.

(a.) Clerks of the Peace.

RECEIPTS OF CLERKS OF THE PEACE.

	£
Salaries and emoluments from Grand Jury cess,	16,775
Fees and emoluments other than from cess or Imperial taxes,	2,361
Received from Imperial taxes,	1,261
Total,	£19,946

(b.) Clerks of the Crown.

RECEIPTS OF CLERKS OF THE CROWN.

	£
Salaries and other payments from Grand Jury cess,	5,460
Emoluments from Imperial taxes,	1,412
Other emoluments,	443
Total,	£6,906

* See note on pages 32 and 33.

(a.) Petty Sessions clerks.

The receipts from Petty Sessions stamps and Crown fines and the application thereof are shown in the following table:—

			£
Receipts.			
Produce of Petty Sessions stamps,	.	.	24,543
Produce of Crown fines,	.	.	27,329
Dividends,	.	.	4,801
Amount transferred from Dogs Act fund,	.	.	26,723
Total,	.	.	£23,484
Application.			
Officers of local courts,	.	.	71,780
Treasurers of Boroughs, and private parties,	.	.	8,151
Royal Irish Constabulary fund,	.	.	1,823
Crime Diseases account,	.	.	158
Total,	.	.	£81,845

4. The Dogs Licence Duty.

The collection of the dogs licence duty is entrusted to the Petty Sessions clerks, and a return of it is made to Parliament by the Registrar of Petty Sessions clerks, so that an abstract only is included in Appendix V. to this Report. A considerable part of the remuneration of Petty Sessions clerks is derived from the dogs licence duty. The surplus of the duty, after providing for the cost of collection, is paid over in aid of Grand Jury cess and Town rates.

			£
Receipts.			
Amount of the Dogs Licence Duty,	.	.	39,971
Dividends,	.	.	350
			£40,374
Application.			
In aid of Grand Jury cess,	.	.	33,807
In aid of Town rates,	.	.	1,179
Cost of postage, &c.,	.	.	36
Deducted and added to Fines and Fees fund, by order of the Lord Lieutenant, under 44 & 45 Vic., c. 14,	.	.	25,186
Total dogs licence duty,	.	.	£40,374

5. Local taxation for Dublin Metropolitan Police.

Taxes similar in principle to those imposed for support of London Metropolitan police:—

		£	£
Rates on houses and land,	.	35,197	
Carriage duty,	.	3,653	
			38,850
Taxes peculiar to Dublin:—			
Pawnbrokers' licenses,	.	4,891	
Publicans' and pedlars' certificates,	.	544	
			5,435
Taxes connected with police courts rather than with police:—			
Fines and penalties from police courts,	.	6,025	
Fees from police courts,	.	1,080	
			6,105
Total,	.	.	£49,671

6. Court Leet Presentments.

It has been ascertained that the only Court Leet in Ireland which has not actually ceased to exist is that in the Manor of Hillsbrogh, including the town of Lisburn, in the county of Antrim, of which an account is given in Appendix XXVI. to the Report for 1869. The Court Leet presentments bore some resemblance to Grand Jury cess in having been levied off land and partly applied towards minor roads; they resembled town taxation in having been applied to town fountains, fire-engines, and fairs and markets. There has been no presentment made for many years, and the Court Leet referred to may be regarded as practically obsolete.

7. Taxation under Harbour Authorities.

The receipts and expenditure of the Harbour Authorities are shown in the following summary:—

Receipts.	£	Expenditure.	£
Import and export tonnage and ballast dues,	168,163	New works and improvements,	54,353
Harbour, port, anchorage, buoy, and tonnage bills,	63,728	Repairs and maintenance of works,	70,569
Pilotage dues,	18,628	Payments in respect of borrowed money,	63,537
Wharf, pier, quay, and dock dues,	48,464	Payments out thereof,	14,164
Receipts not classed,	17,912	Interest, annuities, &c.,	101,851
Rents, use of byeter basin, &c.,	12,985	Wages,	33,481
Lighthouse or floating light dues,	703	Surveys, insurance, &c.,	37,238
Sale of materials,	3,335	Lighting harbours, docks, &c.,	1,454
Money borrowed on bond,	73,734	Rents, rates, taxes, &c.,	5,909
From Imperial taxes,	9,157	Law expenses,	13,470
From Grand Jury cess, or other local tax,	2,444	Repayments through Treasury to Imperial loans,	1,431
		Lighthouses and floating lights,	1,576
		Repayments to Grand Jury cess,	30
Total receipts,	£615,156	Total expenditure,	£461,191

8. Inland Navigations.

These navigations are under the management of Boards of trustees, and are fully described in the Report on local taxation for 1871.

(a.) Maintained out of Grand Jury Cess.

Receipts.	£	Expenditure.	£
From Grand Jury cess,	3,313	Works,	3,308
Tolls,	208	Salaries and incidentals,	943
Other receipts,	64		
Total receipts,	£3,453	Total expenditure,	£4,353

(b.) Maintained out of the Imperial taxes, or by receipts from Tolls, &c.

These navigations are also fully described in the Report for 1871.

Receipts.	£	Expenditure.	£
Parliamentary grant,	318	Works,	3,030
Tolls,	1,944	Salaries and incidentals,	1,351
Receipts not classed,	3,319		
Total receipts,	£5,542	Total expenditure,	£4,351

9. Arterial Drainage.

Repayments for Expenditure on Drainage Works executed by Commissioners of Public Works.

The particulars of these repayments have been supplied by the Commissioners of Public Works. The repayments made by proprietors of lands amounted to £35,710, and the sum repaid out of county cess was £1,944.

10. Receipts and Expenditure of Town Authorities.

The receipts of the various town authorities are grouped together in the following table to facilitate comparison of the amounts collected by the different classes of town authorities. The taxation levied by the Commissioner of the Dublin Metropolitan Police is not included therein, as the expenditure on police is not under the control of local authorities, but is shown separately in the summary table on page 11.

The receipts are divided into—(1) rates on real property; (2) tolls, dues, and fees; (3) from rents and other sources; (4) from borrowed money and the issue of stock; (5) from Imperial taxes; and (6) from Grand Jury cess, or other local tax.

B

RECEIPTS OF TOWN AUTHORITIES.

Sources.	From under Town Councils	Commissioners under special Acts	Towns having Commissioners under Act of 1854	From under Lighting and Cleansing Commissioners	Total Receipts	Per cent.
	£	£	£	£	£	
1. Rates on real property, . .	673,384	144,742	65,419	6,735	878,833	52·25
2. Tolls, and Market charges, Dues, and Fees, . . .	40,533	3,377	5,833	77	49,533	3·03
3. Rents, and other receipts, .	120,579	37,839	21,579	6,193	172,808	13·34
4. From borrowed money and from the issue of Stock, . .	222,789	55,881	37,448	40	317,018	27·35
5. From Parliamentary Grants.	19,353	3,467	1,849	55	24,523	1·03
6. From Grand Jury, or other local taxing Body. . . .	9,393	1,536	3,330	160	14,619	1·11
Total, . .	900,683	273,899	114,054	7,344	1,290,846	100

It appears from this table, that of the total receipts of town authorities in Ireland—£1,205,846—£876,833, or 52·25 per cent., was from rates on real property ; £357,018 or 27·86 per cent., was from money borrowed on the security of the rates and realised by the issue of Stock ; £172,805, or 13·34 per cent., was from rents and other sources ; £49,533, or 3·95 per cent., was from tolls and market charges, dues, and fees ; £24,523, or 1·89 per cent., was from the Imperial taxes ; and £14,419, or 1·11 per cent. was from Grand Jury cess, or other local tax.

(* This includes £19,353 received under the Probate Duties (Scotland and Ireland) Act, 1888, the distribution of which is shown in Table XXI. of the Appendix, page 64.)

EXPENDITURE OF TOWN AUTHORITIES.

Institutions.	Towns under Town Councils	Commissioners under special Acts	Towns having Commissioners under Act of 1854	Towns under Lighting and Cleansing Commissioners	Total expenditure.	Per cent.
	£	£	£	£	£	
Payments in respect of borrowed money, and expenditure contracted, .	342,383	138,180	45,895	3,715	527,043	38·49
Water supply, . . .	82,115	87,338	23,887	637	194,177	14·25
Paving and repairs of streets,	131,771	72,685	10,480	323	164,187	12·23
County charges paid out of Grand Jury cess by Town Councils, and payments in aid of Grand Jury cess, . . .	64,788	16,338	1,995	—	83,003	6·02
Building, demolition of walls, &c.,	61,179	88,170	1,779	—	80,183	4·97
Lighting, including lamps, pipes, &c.,	51,873	6,183	11,648	1,633	71,835	5·27
Making sewers or drains, and other sanitary objects, . .	121,353	19,763	6,730	693	145,146	10·26
Cleansing and watering streets, .	82,749	4,339	4,307	135	91,644	6·73
Watching, . . .	1,679	101	135	134	2,032	·15
Total, .	929,773	416,170	11·,630	7,357	1,362,250	100

11.—Burial Boards.

The receipts and expenditure of Town Authorities for burial ground purposes are included in the town returns; and the details of the receipts and expenditure of rural burial boards, and of the urban burial boards from which returns have been received, and of joint urban and rural burial boards are shown in Table XVI, in the Appendix.

12.—Poor Rates.

The particulars of collection and expenditure of poor rates are fully set forth in the annual Reports of the Local Government Board, and it is only necessary here to refer to abstract XVII, in the Appendix, page 44, in order to ascertain the amount of these rates which is included in the classified summary of local taxation given in the following table.

13. Classification of Local Taxation, and amount received from (1) Rates on Real Property; (2) Tolls, Fees, Stamps, and Dues; and (3) Other Sources.

Excluding borrowed money and grants from Imperial taxes, the local taxation of Ireland in 1898 is classified in the following table to show how much was obtained, respectively, from rates on real property, from tolls fees stamps and dues, and from other sources of receipt.

In the case of Grand Jury taxation it is necessary to deduct from the other receipts given on page 16, £18,907, received from the Dogs Licence duty, and £2,518 produced by the sale of investments, while as regards town taxation the following deductions must be made from the receipts from other sources of £172,303, included in the table on the opposite page:—£5,028 received from Petty Sessions Stamps and Crown fines, £1,178 from the Dogs Licence duty, £4,107 from grants or contributions made for specific purposes, and sums amounting to £18,207 which either appear twice in the accounts of the same authority, or are accumulations of sinking funds applied in discharge of debt, thereby reducing the amount of such receipts to £113,291.

Classified summary of local taxation, exclusive of moneys first Loan, and from Imperial Taxes.	Rates on real property.	Tolls, Fees, Stamps, and Dues.	Other sources.	Total amount of local taxation.
	£	£	£	£
1. Grand Jury cess	1,221,721		14,051	1,234,782
2. Fees of Clerks of the Peace		2,302	—	4,201
3. Fees of Clerks of the Crown		143	—	143
4. Petty Sessions stamps and Crown fines	—	61,871	3,851	81,723
5. Dogs licence duty		39,974	360	40,334
6. Dublin Metropolitan Police taxes	36,197	10,420	3,860	43,577
7. Quart Land presentments	—			
8. Harbour taxation (exclusive of customs rates, &c.)	—	154,173	493,103	357,373
9. Inland navigation taxation	—	2,175	4,303	3,466
10. Town taxation (exclusive of receipts from Dogs Licence duty, Fines, grants for specific purposes, Grand Jury cess, &c., as above)	678,033	44,534	143,291	870,057
11. Burial board receipts other than from rates (exclusive of sums received by urban burial boards)	—	1,446	143	1,589
12. Poor rate and other receipts of Boards of Guardians (exclusive of repayment of relief, and of the burial board receipts included in No. 11)	1,606,383	—	65,770	1,672,153
13. Light dues, and fees under Merchant Shipping Act	—	19,474	—	19,474
Total, { 1898	3,388,104	674,634	871,820	4,697,918
{ 1899	3,525,902	671,886	286,271	3,500,238
Increase,	112,112	2,367	—	107,710
Decrease,	—	—	18,860	—

It appears from the foregoing table that the amount of the local taxation of Ireland in the year 1893 was produced as follows :—

	£	Per cent.
Rates on real property produced,	8,883,104	or 79·83 of the total amount.
Tolls, Fees, Stamps, and Dues,	876,838	„ 17·82 „ „
Other receipts,	871,510	„ 7·35 „ „
Total,	**£3,697,940**	**100**

As compared with the revised taxation of the previous year which is given at foot of the table on the preceding page, there was, therefore, an increase of £119,112 in the amount produced by "Rates on real property," and of £3,167 in that produced by "Tolls, Fees, Stamps, and Dues," while there was a decrease of £13,569 in that by "Other receipts," making a net increase of £107,710, as already shown on pages 5 and 6 of this Report.

APPENDICES.

APPENDICES TO REPORT ON

I.—SUMMARY of Grand Jury Cess authorised to be levied in the year 1893 in each County, and County of Grand Juries, and by the City Accountant, or Borough Treasurer.

COUNTIES AND COUNTIES OF CITIES AND OF TOWNS, &c.)	Roads and Bridges		Repairs of Damages done by Floods	Baronial Rents	Public Institutions			Indemnities, Repayment of Advances and Incidental Charges
	New	Repairs			Prisons and Lunatic Asylums	Other expenses	Lunatic Asylums, &c. Repayment of Advances	
	£	£	£	£	£	£	£	£
Antrim, ...						-		
Armagh, ...						-		
Carlow, ...						-		
Carrickfergus, Co. of the Town, . .					-	-		
Cavan, ...						-		
Clare, ...						-		
Cork, ...						-		
Cork, County of the City, . .		-				-		
Donegal, ...						-		
Down, ...			-			?		
Drogheda, County of the Town, . .						-		
Dublin, ...						-		
Dublin, County of the City, . .	-	-					-	
Fermanagh, ...						-		
Galway, ...						-		
Galway, County of the Town, . .	-					-		
Kerry, ...						-		
Kildare, ...						-		
Kilkenny, ...	-					-		
Kilkenny, County of the City, . .						-		
King's County, ...						-		
Leitrim, ...						-		
Limerick, ...						-		
Limerick, County of the City, . .	-	-				-		
Londonderry, ...						-		
Louth, &c.						-		
Louth, ...						-		
Mayo, ...						-		
Meath, ...						-		
Monaghan, ...						-		
Queen's County, ...						-		
Roscommon, ...						-		
Sligo, ...			-			-		
Tipperary, North Riding, . .						-		
Tipperary, South Riding, . .						-		
Tyrone, ...						-		
Waterford, ...						-		
Waterford, County of the City, . .						-		
Wexford, ...						-		
Wicklow, ...			-			-		
Total, . .								

* The local grants of the Grand Juries of the Counties of the Cities of Cork, Dublin, and Limerick are vested in the Municipal Authority of the City.

of a city and County of a town, compiled from returns furnished by County Treasurers, Secretaries in the case of the Counties of the cities of Cork, Dublin, and Limerick.*

											COUNTIES AND COUNTIES OF CITIES AND OF TOWNS.

In each case, also the amount of the loans in lieu of Grand Jury Cesspresentment in the preceding half year...

11.—Summary showing the amount of Grand Jury Cess, and other receipts, in each County by the Auditors of the

during the year 1892, with the expenditure thereof, prepared from the abstracts furnished
Local Government Board.

II.—Summary of returns made by Clerks of the Peace, of salaries, emoluments, and fees

COUNTIES, AND COUNTIES OF CITIES AND OF TOWNS.	Salary.	Emoluments				Fees paid by Crown Solicitors.
		Compensation paid (Clerical, Justices' Act, and other payments from Imperial taxes)	Payments by sureties to discharge Prosecutors' Fines, &c.	Fees.	Other Emoluments from Grand Jury, &c.	
	£ s. d.	£ s. d.	£ s. d.	£ s. d.	£ s. d.	£ s. d.
Antrim, ...		4 5 0			–	
Belfast, Borough of, . .		–			–	
Carrickfergus, Co. of the Town,		–			–	
Clare, ...		–			–	
Donegal, ...						
Dublin, ...						
Dublin, County of the City,		–				
Galway, ...		–			–	
Galway, County of the Town,		–			–	
Kilkenny, ...					–	
Kilkenny, County of the City,					–	
Leitrim, ...						
Monaghan, ...					–	
Tyrone, ...					–	
Waterford, ...					–	
Waterford, County of the City,		–			–	
Wexford, ...					–	
Total, - {1849} {1850}						
Increase, . .					–	
Decrease, . .						

received by them, under statute, custom, or other authority, during the year 1893.

							COUNTIES AND COUNTIES OF CITIES AND OF TOWNS.
£ s. d.	£ s. d.	£ s. d.	£ s. d.	£ s. d.	£ s. d.	£ s. d.	
						1,35_ 0 0	Antrim.
		-			-	1,33_ 0 0	Belfast, Borough of.
		-			-	_ 0 0	Carrickfergus, Co. of the Town.
					-	_ 0 0	Clare.
					-	1,_7 0 0	Donegal.
					-	1,43_ 0 0	Dublin.
						1,_ 0 0	Dublin, County of the City.
					-	1,_ 0 0	Galway.
-			-	-	-	_7_ 0 0	Galway, County of the Town.
-			-	-	-	_ 0 0	Kilkenny.
-			-	-	-	_ 0 0	Kilkenny, County of the City.
-			-	-	-	_ 0 0	Leitrim.
			-	-	-	_ 0 0	Roscommon.
			-	-	-	1,_7_ 0 0	Tyrone.
			-	-		_ 0 0	Wexford.
		-	-	-		_ 0 0	Waterford, Co. of the City.
			-	-	-	_ 0 0	Westmeath.
						14,_ 0 0	Total.
						_ 0 0	
	-			-			Leinster.
-		-	-		_ 0 0	_ 0 0	Munster.

III.—SUMMARY of returns of fees and other emoluments received by Clerks of the Crown under patents, customs, or other authority, as sworn to by them at Spring and Summer Assizes of the year 1830, under Statute 6 & 7 Wm. IV., c. 116, s. 112, including presentments for salaries.

COUNTIES, AND COUNTIES OF CITIES AND OF TOWNS.	Salary.	Fees paid by the Grand Jury Cess.	Fees paid by Sheriffs, Bailiffs, and others presentment of Crown Court.	Fees other than those paid by County Treasurer.	Fees and emoluments not classified.	Total amount of all sums, fees, and emoluments received.
	£ s. d.	£ s. d.	£ s. f.	£ s. d.	£ s. d.	£ s. d.
Antrim, ...					—	
Carrickfergus, County of the Town,		—			—	
Clare, ...		—			—	
Donegal, ...		—			—	
Dublin, ...		—			—	
Dublin, County of the City, .	—	—			—	
Galway, ...		—			—	
Galway, County of the Town, .		—			—	
Kilkenny, ...		—			—	
Kilkenny, County of the City,		—			—	
Louth, ...		—			—	
Monaghan, ...		—			—	
Tyrone, ...		—			—	
Wexford, ...		—			—	
Waterford, County of the City,		—			—	
Westmeath, ...		—	—		—	
Total, { Irish. { British.					—	
	—				—	—

IV.—SUMMARY of Petty Sessions stamps and Crown fines, with their application.

RECEIPTS IN 1871.		£ s. d.	APPLICATION IN 1893.		£ s. d.	£ s. d.
Petty Sessions stamps,		24,643 0 0	Officers of local courts—			
Fines,			Salaries of Petty Sessions Clerks,	20,594 0 0		
Less on portion on costs,			Petty Sessions Pay-schedules Clerks,	4,144 0 0		
Christmas,			Salaries of Registrar and his Clerks,	4,144 0 0		
Amount transferred from Dogs Act fund,			expenses, &c.,	2,344 0 0	71,344 0 0	
			Police—			
			Dublin Metropolitan,		1,476 0 0	
			Royal Irish Constabulary,		1,476 0 0	
			Criminal prosecutions,			
			V. Executive of hundreds,		2,191 0 0	
			Private papers,			
		£33,114 0 0			£33,114 0 0	

V.—SUMMARY of Dogs Licence Duty, and its application.

RECEIPTS IN 1893.		£ s. d.	APPLICATION IN 1893.		£ s. d.
Dogs licence duty,		39,674 0 0	Cost of postage, &c.,		64 0 0
Sixbands on money borrowed,		200 0 0	In aid of County Jury men,		13,797 0 0
			In aid of Poor rates,		1,170 0 0
			Balances paid added to Fines and Fees Fund, by order of the Lord Lieutenant, under 44 & 45 Vic., s. 34,		33,134 0 0
		£40,334 0 0			£40,334 0 0

VI.—SUMMARY of special local taxes received by the Dublin Metropolitan Police Commissioner for year ended the 31st of March, 1894.

REVENUE.		£ s. d.	EXPENDITURE.		£ s. d.
Sums received under Contributions:—			Paid into Treasury in aid of cost of Metropolitan police,		33,196 0 0
Dublin Metropolitan Police tax,	32,653 0 0	33,197 0 0			
Carriage duty,	1,197 0 0				
Pawnbrokers' licences,	624 0 0				
Publicans' and Publicans' certificates,	1,393 0 0				
Poor-house Police money,		14,634 0 0			
		2,433 0 0			
Fees and Penalties from Police courts,		32,071 0 0			
Total from taxation,					
Instalments, pay of police specially employed, sale of cast clothing, &c.,		1,444 0 0			
Total amount applicable in reduction of expenditure,		33,149 0 0	Total,		33,149 0 0

VII.—COURT LEET PRESENTMENTS in Manor of Killultagh, including town of Lisburn.

		£ s. d.
Total amount presented on separate Constablewicks,		—
in Manor at large,		—
Total presented,		—
Total amount levied,		—

VIII.—Summary of Dues, Tolls, Rents, and other Receipts of Harbour and Pier Authorities, for the

VIII. (continued).—SUMMARY of expenditure of Harbour and Pier Authorities, for the latest

Name of Authority, Port, Pier, Quay, or Wharf.		Expenditure.							
Annalong,		12	—	—	3	—	—	—	—
Ardglass,	—	140	—	—	346	—	—	—	—
Arklow,	—	71	940	—	317	—	—	—	—
Ballycastle,	—	40	64	—	14	—	—	11	—
Ballina,	—	90	—	675	523	—	—	—	—
Ballycotton,	—	90	—	—	9	—	—	—	—
Baltimore and Skibbereen,	—	117	1	—	6	—	4	—	6
Belfast Harbour and Docks,	—	7,370	—	11,444	53,582	343	—	2,644	3,735
Bundoran Pier,	—	—	—	—	1	—	—	—	—
Carlingford Lough,	—	340	143	—	173	—	204	—	36
Carrickfergus,	—	63	141	—	143	—	—	60	39
Clew Circle,	—	84	5	—	10	—	—	11	—
Colraine,	443	141	133	32	117	—	—	70	—
Cork,	—	3,341	4,474	1,480	3,439	—	1,345	330	1,387
Courtown,	—	—	143	—	20	—	30	1	3
Dingle,	—	71	4	—	31	10	—	—	3
Donaghadee,	—	45	—	—	270	—	—	—	—
Dingloss,	—	571	440	1,471	1,431	—	—	630	41
Dublin,	—	4,433	1,710	1,443	63,380	1,473	133	—	4,141
Do. Custom House Docks,	—	3,330	3,740	—	3,044	—	—	340	3,444
Dundalk,	—	611	1,183	113	743	—	448	63	714
Dunfanaghy,	—	—	—	—	1	—	—	—	—
Dungarvan, including Ballinacourty, Ballinacourt, and Helvick,	—	63	64	—	—	—	44	—	1
Ennismore East, Harbour, Pier, and Dock,	—	145	—	—	300	—	—	—	—
Fermoy,	—	63	—	51	7	—	—	—	6
Galway,	—	343	493	—	333	—	—	90	41
Howth,	—	103	—	—	343	—	—	—	30
Killybegs Pier,	14	9	—	—	29	—	—	—	—
Kilrush Quay and Harbour,	—	9	1	—	—	—	—	—	—
Kilrush Pier and Harbour,	—	30	—	—	—	—	1	6	—
Kingstown,	—	440	—	344	4,344	—	—	340	—
Kinsale,	—	30	63	—	37	—	—	14	34
Larne,	—	1,944	1,340	—	3,370	—	—	40	344
Limerick,	433	1,130	794	3,340	1,433	—	1,343	543	343
Londonderry,	—	3,341	9,444	3,330	3,794	—	340	1,477	340
Magheramore Pier,	—	6	—	—	—	—	—	—	—
New Ross,	640	330	770	—	—	—	—	—	6
Queenstown,	40	33	—	—	—	—	—	—	—
Skerries,	—	30	44	—	10	—	—	—	36
Sligo,	—	340	630	3,371	433	40	30	140	340
Tralee and Fenit,	—	340	440	10	443	—	343	43	33
Waterford, including Arthurstown, Ballyhack, and Duncannon,	333	1,344	3,344	—	3,111	331	374	340	64
Westport,	—	340	443	133	643	—	43	—	63
Wexford,	—	493	1,344	344	3,744	—	340	343	341
Wicklow,	—	31	433	—	—	44	—	—	—
Youghal,	—	39	73	49	34	—	—	440	9
Total,	3,340	33,343	33,494	33,343	79,430	3,034	4,444	3,434	13,473

* See note 30, where prefixed

period of twelve months for which the accounts were made up preceding 31st December, 1882.

									Name of Harbour, Port, Pier, Quay, or Wharf.
£	£	£	£	£	£	£	£	£	
-	-	-	-	-	-	-	14	149	148	Arranmore
-	-	-	-	-	-	-	-	268	438	Antrim
-	-	19	-	-	-	9	479	92	699	Arklow
-	-	-	-	-	-	10	250	7	311	Ballycotton
715	-	-	-	-	-	119	1,437	874	3,121	Ballina
-	-	-	-	-	-	-	6	12	61	Ballyronan
1,123	-	-	-	-	-	32	679	37	244	Baltimore and Skibbereen
1,681	64,997	-	-	-	-	16,983	184,969	96,849	332,429	Belfast Harbour and Docks
-	-	-	-	-	-	-	4	16	20	Bundoran Pier
-	768	-	-	-	-	875	3,585	97	1,414	Collingford Lough
1,291	763	-	-	-	-	48	3,368	859	9,045	Coolfahertyca
-	-	-	-	-	-	-	66	154	479	Glass Oask
1,489	694	147	-	-	-	368	3,489	-	3,289	Coleraine
-	13,589	489	-	-	-	7,185	38,884	14,390	68,445	Cork
16	-	-	-	-	-	11	788	84	388	Courtown
-	-	-	-	-	-	34	148	-	343	Drogheda
-	-	-	-	-	-	-	544	-	343	Dingle
-	951	9	-	-	-	1,389	3,447	1,389	4,387	Dundalk
-	17,651	797	-	-	-	3,174	38,385	3,385	40,389	Dublin
-	-	41	-	-	-	1,389	14,889	3,389	34,389	Do. Custom House Docks
-	4,489	-	-	-	-	469	3,464	1,346	7,388	Dundalk
-	-	-	-	-	-	-	4	4	7	Dunfanaghy
149	-	-	-	-	-	36	898	-	989	Dungarvan
-	-	-	-	-	-	-	348	-	666	Dungannon East
89	84	-	-	-	-	33	788	-	779	Fenit
780	489	-	-	-	-	39	3,384	3,389	3,384	Galway
-	-	-	-	-	-	-	889	-	489	Howth
-	-	-	-	-	-	-	96	-	66	Kilkelyport Pier
98	4	-	-	-	-	9	89	9	34	Kilrush Quay and Harbour
-	-	-	-	-	-	86	96	469	899	Kilrush Pier and Harbour
-	-	-	-	-	-	-	6,389	-	6,389	Kingstown
689	-	-	-	-	-	49	689	48	667	Kinsale
889	1,94	-	-	-	-	-	3,984	1,489	3,774	Larne
-	4,789	89	-	-	-	889	13,440	489	73,138	Limerick
74,989	6,389	889	-	-	-	3,714	98,489	64,889	Londonderry
-	-	-	-	-	-	9	9	39	79	Mountcharles Pier
9	1,46	17	-	-	-	49	989	-	1,389	New Ross
-	-	-	-	-	-	-	19	9	49	Queenstown
-	-	6	-	-	-	-	89	389	689	Skerries
789	1,481	-	-	-	-	6,989	34,889	739	14,789	Sligo
849	-	-	-	-	-	669	3,388	49	3,389	Tralee and Fenit
849	913	489	-	-	-	3,711	73,949	-	33,489	Waterford
689	31	-	-	-	-	849	3,489	489	3,389	Westport
-	889	14	-	-	-	1,449	4,389	389	3,489	Wexford
-	-	-	-	84	-	889	744	-	364	Wicklow
-	199	-	-	-	-	49	869	989	689	Youghal
84,439	199,839	3,483	-	89	-	64,389	489,489	389,389	889,844	Total

IX.—SUMMARY of tolls and other income, with expenditure, in respect of Inland Navigations.

Name of Navigation	Balance in favour at the commencement of the financial year	Income				Balance against at the close of the financial year	Total
		Superintendence	Tolls	Annual amounts	Total income during the year		
	£ s. d.	£ s. d.	£ s. d.	£ s. d.	£ s. d.	£ s. d.	£ s. d.
Lough Corrib	—	213 0 0	64 0 0	—	846 0 0	0 0 0	243 0 0
Lower Bann	695 0 0	1,500 0 0	54 0 0	3 0 0	2,130 0 0	267 0 0	1,500 0 0
Upper Bann	72 0 0	204 0 0	140 0 0	64 0 0	1,420 0 0	—	1,500 0 0
Total	767 0 0	2,324 0 0	258 0 0	64 0 0	5,002 0 0	273 0 0	4,432 0 0

X.—SUMMARY of tolls and other receipts, with expenditure, in respect of Inland Navigations maintained out of local period for which the accounts were made

Name of Navigation	Balance in favour at the close of the financial year	Income					Balance against at the close of the financial year	Total
		Superintendence	Annual duty	Tolls	Other charges	Total receipts during the year		
	£ s. d.	£ s. d.	£ s. d.	£ s. d.	£ s. d.	£ s. d.	£ s. d.	£ s. d.
Lower Bann	—	800 0 0	—	837 0 0	—	433 0 0	—	433 0 0
Maigue (County Limerick)	—	10 0 0	—	35 0 0	—	59 0 0	—	59 0 0
Shannon	—	—	—	1,331 0 0	3,310 0 0	3,430 0 0	1,831 0 0	4,831 0 0
Total	—	810 0 0	—	1,300 0 0	3,310 0 0	4,483 0 0	1,831 0 0	7,390 0 0
Total of IX. and X.	767 0 0	613 0 0	1,300 0 0	1,373 0 0	3,483 0 0	3,884 0 0	2,334 0 0	11,434 0 0

XI.—SUMMARY of repayments of expenditure for Arterial drainage made to the Commissioners of Public ... &c., during the year ended

—	Total Expenditure by Board of Works chargeable on Lands and Counties	Portion charged on Baronly sums	Portion charged on lands improved	Charge per annum
	£ s. d.	£ s. d.	£ s. d.	£ s. d.
Under 5 & 6 Vic., c. 89, and Acts amending same	1,344,693 0 0	106,831 0 0	642,377 0 0	—
Cases 26 & 27 Vic., c. 88	504,693 0 0	42,807 0 0	704,840 0 0	12,809 0 0
Under 44 & 45 Vic., c. 49, Maintenance works	63,130 0 0	—	63,130 0 0	—
Total	1,932,131 1 1	208,379 0 0	1,792,837 0 0	12,809 0 0

maintained out of Grand Jury cess, for the year 1878, from returns by Navigation trustees.

Amount received at the commencement of the financial year.	Expenditure.			Surplus in hand at the close of the financial year.	Total.	Name of Navigation
	Works.	Salaries and Incidentals.	Total.			
£ s. d.	£ s. d.	£ s. d.	£ s. d.	£ s. d.	£ s. d.	
4 0 0	184 0 0	159 0 0	346 0 0	—	350 0 0	Lough Corrib.
—	3,340 0 0	417 0 0	2,803 0 0	—	3,800 0 0	Lower Bann.
—	737 0 0	173 0 0	909 0 0	879 0 0	1,791 0 0	Upper Bann.
4 0 0	3,860 0 0	343 0 0	4,153 0 0	876 0 0	4,890 0 0	Total.

of the Imperial taxes, or by receipts from tolls, &c., for twelve months ended the 31st of March, 1883, the up previous to the 31st of December, 1882.

Balance carried at the commencement of the financial year.	Expenditure.			Surplus payable to the Exchequer.	Balance in favour at the close of the financial year.	Total.	Name of Navigation.
	Works.	Salaries and Incidentals.	Total.				
£ s. d.	£ s. d.	£ s. d.	£ s. d.	£ s. d.	£ s. d.	£ s. d.	
—	102 0 0	142 0 0	700 0 0	190 0 0	—	400 0 0	Lower Boyne.
—	5 0 0	17 0 0	10 0 0	10 0 0	—	50 0 0	Maigue (County Limerick)
1,844 0 0	2,400 0 0	1,200 0 0	3,607 0 0	—	—	6,811 0 0	Shannon.
7,844 0 0	6,800 0 0	1,301 0 0	4,368 0 0	246 0 0	—	7,380 0 0	Total.
3,840 0 0	4,800 0 0	2,140 0 0	3,604 0 0	126 0 0	170 0 0	11,600 0 0	Total of IX. and X.

Works, under 5 & 6 Vic., c. 89, and Acts amending same, and under 26 & 27 Vic., c. 88, and 29 & 30 Vic., the 31st of March, 1894.

Total appropriated during year.	Portion of appropriation out by loss of County cess during year.	Repayments made by proprietors of lands during year.	—
£ s. d.	£ s. d.	£ s. d.	
110 0 0	—	170 0 0	Under 5 & 6 Vic., c. 89, and Acts amending same.
60,000 0 0	1,844 0 0	35,000 0 0	Under 26 & 27 Vic., c. 88.
1,800 0 0	—	1,800 0 0	Under 29 & 30 Vic., c. 49, Arterial Drainage works.
57,000 0 0	1,844 0 0	64,710 0 0	Total.

XII.—Summary of returns of all sums received by Town Councils
the financial year

Part I.—Receipts

Part II.—Expenditure

under statute, charter, or other authority, and of the expenditure thereof, for
ended in 1893.

with the exception of Waterford which assumed the charter of Incorporation in 1893.

during financial year.

Towns and county Districts, under name of Townships (all Towns and Boroughs.)	Sessions under which Acts are passed.	Balance in hands at the commencement of the year.		Receipts.	
			Legislative and Rates.	Other Rates.	From Mortgages, Fines, &c.
LEICESTER.		£	£	£	£
Boston City :					
Fire-Office-square (Commissioners), . . .	59 Geo. III., c. 163,	No power.	–	–	–
Horrise-square (Commissioners), . . .	51 Geo. III., c. 45 (Lo.) and 49 Geo. III., c. 62 (Pr.) s. 18.	No power.	–	–	–
Montpilor-square (Commissioners), . . .	59 Geo. III., c. 91.	No power.	–	–	–
Railroad-square (Governors of Leamington Hospital), .	65 Geo. III., c. 44.	–	–	101	–
Dublin County :					
Blackrock Township (Commissioners), . .	26 & 27 Vic., c. 21.	15	5,302	2,519	–
Clontarf Ditto, ...	61 & 62 Vic., c. 65,	650	1,654	1,679	–
Dalkey Ditto, ...	60 & 61 Vic., c. 146,	816	2,620	–	–
Drumcondra, Clonliffe, and Glasnevin Township (Commissioners),	41 & 42 Vic., c. 187,	–	1,527	–	–
Kingstown (Town) Ditto, . .	31 & 32 Vic., c. 116,	–	1,649	–	–
Kilmaine Ditto, ...	62 & 63 Vic., c. 213, and other Acts.	65	14,258	1,654	9
Pembroke Ditto, ...	66 & 67 Vic., c. 97, and 68 & 69 Vic., c. 66.	–	20,657	–	–
Rathmines and Rathgar Township (Improvement Commissioners),	62 & 63 Vic., c. 227, 68 & 69 Vic., c. 187, and 62 & 63 Vic., c. 125.	3,654	25,215	–	–
Wicklow County and Dublin County :					
Bray Township (Commissioners), . . .	22 & 23 Vic., c. 272, and 24 & 25 Vic., c. 140.	3,152	5,707	659	140
ULSTER.					
Belfast City and Harbor, West Commissioners,	47 & 48 Vic., c. 360; 50 & 51 Vic., c. 276.	27,877	–	14,691	–
Carrickfergus (Municipal Commissioners), .	6 & 7 Vic., c. 102; and 8 & 9 Vic., c. 69.	652	–	–	67
Enniskillen (Commissioners of the Borough), .	38 & 39 Vic., c. 142.	600	1,159	634	–
Newry (Commissioners), ...	56 & 57 Vic., c. 350.	1,672	4,689	1,657	1,659
CONNAUGHT.					
Galway Town (Improvement Commissioners), .	16 & 17 Vic., c. 299,	–	721	3,654	1,264
Total. . . . . { 1859		79,569	65,613	39,759	4,657
{ 1858		51,657	54,558	33,564	5,759
Increase.		38,564	1,154	4,505	67
Decrease.		–	–	–	–

having powers of local taxation under special Acts, and in one case (Carrickfergus) by Municipal
for the financial year ended in 1892.

during financial year.

Expenses								Towns and county Districts, showing in Parenthesis (if Towns and Numbers).
£	£	£	£	£	£	£	£	
								LEINSTER.
								Dublin City :
...	...	...	...	...	...	...	...	[illegible] (Commissioners).
...	...	...	...	...	...	...	...	[illegible] (Commissioners).
...	...	...	...	...	...	...	...	[illegible] (Commissioners).
...	...	...	...	...	164	...	...	[illegible] (Governors of [illegible] Hospital).
								Dublin County :
64	6,450	354	637	140	23,450	...	31,450	[illegible] Township (Commissioners).
...	4,050	...	157	62	6,350	...	4,050	[illegible] Dist.
90	...	...	72	91	4,575	...	3,550	[illegible] Dist.
...	500	30	550	74	5,775	...	5,350	[illegible], and [illegible] Township (Commissioners).
...	250	...	165	440	6,460	450	5,350	[illegible] (New) Dist.
61	3,501	103	440	540	33,790	...	33,440	[illegible] Dist.
...	5,450	...	645	3,315	39,407	5,234	67,400	[illegible] Dist.
144	49,154	...	575	6,451	64,550	...	57,904	[illegible] and [illegible] Township (Improvement Commissioners).
								Wicklow County and Dublin County :
74	30,350	...	154	577	50,450	...	32,770	[illegible] Township (Commissioners).
								ULSTER.
60	49,570	873	4,354	63,450	...	148,554	[illegible] City and Docks, West (Commissioners).
300	...	...	30	954	3,450	...	3,464	[illegible] (Municipal Commissioners).
540	1,450	...	164	154	4,450	450	5,457	[illegible] (Commissioners of the Borough).
340	...	...	302	554	3,450	...	13,450	[illegible] (Commissioners).
								CONNAUGHT.
9	650	...	140	440	6,575	450	6,150	Galway Town (Improvement Commissioners).
1,470	90,505	1,554	6,454	14,450	787,450	1,450	640,450	[illegible] Fund.
1,554	140,350	454	4,454	45,450	780,750	1,450	450,450	[illegible] Fund.
144	...	753	...	...	...	450	...	[illegible]
...	45,554	...	1,454	65,150	77,350	...	55,772	[illegible]

[XIII. (continued.)

XIII. (continued).—COMMISSIONERS UNDER SPECIAL ACTS. SUMMARY of returns of expenditure by Municipal Commissioners under 3 and 4 Vic., c. 108.

PART II.—Expenditure.

Towns and their Boards (as before and hereafter)	Commissioners under Acts set forth	Balance allowed at the commencement of the year	of Sums by Liabilities or final effects of Sewers, Wells, Springs, &c.	Paving and Repair of Streets	Cleansing and Watering	Lighting, Scavenging, Lamps, Lamp posts, &c	Watching
		£	£	£	£	£	£
LEINSTER							
OFFALY CO. :							
...	3 Geo. IIL, c. 108.	No return.		-	-	-	-
...	3 Geo. III., c. 44 (Ir.); and 48 Geo. III., c. 69 (Ir.), c. 13.	No return.	-	-	-	-	-
...	3 Geo. III., c. 44.	No return.	-	-	-	-	-
...	3 Geo. III., c. 63.	-	11	-	-	121	-
PHILIP CO. :							
...	39 & 37 Vic., c. 221.	-	1,442	1,272	604	660	-
...	37 & 38 Vic., c. 44.	-	3,422	1,740	223	688	-
...	40 & 44 Vic., c. 128.	-	884	344	60	44	-
...	41 & 42 Vic., c. 102.	648	-	1,206	644	846	-
...	41 & 42 Vic., c. 112.	874	-	744	-	887	-
...	39 & 38 Vic., c. 203, and other Acts.	-	124	1,471	460	268	-
...	38 & 41 Vic., c. 13, and 40 Vic., c. 54 ; and 41 & 42 Vic., c. 103.	4,871	4,280	8,082	-	2,481	-
...		-	1,131	4,280	1,414	1,481	-
WICKLOW COUNTY AND BRAY COUNTY :							
...	34 & 35 Vic., c. 201; and 35 & 36 Vic. c. 93.	-	11,111	440	464	484	-
ULSTER							
...	37 & 38 Vic., c. 102 ; and 39 & 40 Vic., c. 93.	-	-	-	-	-	-
...	3 & 4 Vic., c. 108 ; and 4 & 5 Vic., c. 61.	-	-	-	76	144	-
...	38 & 39 Vic., c. 112.	-	1,464	648	848	868	-
...	34 & 35 Vic., c. 108.	-	4,489	3,488	488	848	-
CONNAUGHT							
Galway Town (Improvement Commrs.)	43 & 47 Vic., c. 108.	4,39	-	1,842	-	4,49	148
Total . . . &c.		1,489	83,778	88,846	4,889	8,788	888
		78,884	84,484	88,488	8,848	7,888	184
Boroughs,		-	84,888	8,488	-	-	-
Commrs.,		4,488	-	-	48	4,478	88

Commissioners having powers of local taxation under special Acts, and in one case (Carrickfergus) by section 16, for the financial year ended in 1893.

during financial year.

									Town and owner amount allowed of Payments. (If Towns and Townships.)
£	£	£	£	£	£	£	£	£	LEINSTER.
									Dublin City :
...	...	—	...	...	...	...	...	...	Pembroke—area (Commissioners).
...	...	...	...	...	...	...	...	...	Kanturk—area (Commissioners).
...	...	—	...	...	...	...	...	...	Rathgar—area (Commissioners).
...	...	...	...	...	199	904	...	994	Rathmines—area (Governor of Lying-in Hospital).
									Dublin County :
600	4,000	000	1,400	3,571	4,300	30,000	300	36,000	Blackrock Township (Commissioners).
000	01	00	300	700	000	4,007	300	4,000	Clontarf Ditto.
304	00	00	300	1,300	371	3,000	304	3,300	Dalkey Ditto.
304	300	315	470	1,743	304	3,000	40	6,136	Dundrum, Clogillie, and Glasnevin Townp. (Commissioners).
000	314	00	000	334	000	1,300		1,300	Kilmainham (New) Ditto.
1,000	371	1,300	3,301	4,000	4,300	30,000	400	30,000	Kingstown Ditto.
4,071	4,034	000	3,354	3,330	3,000	43,004	—	30,000	Pembroke Ditto.
1,000	3,400	1,300	3,415	30,371	11,400	44,300	13,000	67,000	Rathmines and Rathgar Township (Township Commissioners).
									Waterford County and Dublin County :
710	00	000	400	3,300	1,374	30,304	4,000	30,170	Bray Township (Commissioners).

Town Commissioners under Towns Improvement (Ireland) Act, 1854 (17 and 18 Vic. c. 103) for the period in 1893.

XIV. (continued).—SUMMARY of Returns of Receipts and Expenditure of Town Commissioners under

Towns Improvement (Ireland) Act, 1854 (17 & 18 Vic, c. 103), for the financial year ended in 1893.

IV.—LIGHTING AND CLEANSING COMMISSIONERS. Summary of Receipts and Expenditure of Lighting

APPENDICES TO REPORT ON

XVI.—Receipts and Expenditure of Burial Boards

Note—This table, which has been compiled from returns received from Clerks to Burial Boards, does not

during the financial year ended in 1893.

include the name of any Board which has been returned as having no receipts or expenditure during the year.

Boards during the financial year ended in 1893.

XVII.—ABSTRACT showing the receipts and expenditure of Unions in Ireland during the year ended the 29th of September, 1862, exclusive of receipts and payments under the Seed Potatoes Supply Acts, 1880–1881.

Receipts	£	Expenditure	£
Poor Rate levied.		In-Maintenance.	
Parliamentary Grants.		Out-Relief.	
Other receipts.		Reimbursement of Diet and Beef and Sunk to Inmates, and cost of order to various hospitals.	
Loans.		Salaries and rations of officers.	
		Superannuation.	
		All other Poor Relief expenses.	
		Total Poor Relief expenditure.	
		Medical Charities, Vaccination, and Dispensary Houses Acts.	
		Lunatic Asylums Act.	
		Acts for Registration of Births, Deaths, and Marriages.	
		Sanitary Acts.	
		Burial Grounds Acts.	
		Contagious Diseases (Animals) Acts.	
		Payment under National School Teachers Act.	
		Labourers Act.	
		Parliamentary Deposition Acts.	
		Rates and Subvention Acts.	
		Repayment of Loans.	
Total,		Total expenditure,	

* This includes £_____ received under the Pauper Rates (Ireland and Scotland) Act, 1862.

XIX.—SUMMARY of Returns of Debt incurred by, and outstanding against, the various Town and Harbour

Loans Authorities	At the per Cent. of interest, if above 4¼ per Cent.		At Four per Cent., and from 4¼ per Cent.		At Four per Cent., and below Four per Cent.		Below Four per Cent.		On account.	
	No. amount of years.	All amount of years.	No. amount of years.	All amount of years.	No. amount of years.	All amount of years.	No. amount of years.	All amount of years.	No. amount of years.	All amount of years.
I.—Towns UNDER Commissioners										
Total,										
II. Towns and various Commissioners under Sanitary Acts.										
Total,										

XVIII.—SUMMARY of returns of fees received under the Merchant Shipping Act, 1854, during the latest period of twelve months for which the accounts were made up preceding the 31st of December, 1893.

XIX.—SUMMARY of returns of taxation on pawnbrokers by fees received by the City Marshal and by auctioneers of forfeited pledges in the City of Dublin, in the year 1893.

Authorities in Ireland, showing rates of interest paid, and amount of principal paid off during year ended in 1893.

XX.—(continued).—Summary of Returns of Debt incurred by, and outstanding against, the various Town
year ended in

Loan Accounts										

and Harbour Authorities in Ireland, showing rates of interest paid, and amount of principal paid off during 1892—*continued.*

XXII.—Table showing the towns in Ireland which are not Urban Sanitary Districts; the population and valuation of each; its area in acres; and the Acts under which the towns are constituted.

Total number of such towns, . . . 55.

TOWN	Population	Valuation in tons	Area in Acres	Acts under which constituted
Aaron, . . .	1,340	6,640	687	15 and 16 Vic., cap. 105.
Aries, . . .	4,284	3,047	1,240	do.
Arklow, . . .	4,570	4,654	1,302	do.
Athy, . . .	4,640	4,205	301	do.

Dublin Castle,

23rd November, 1894.

Sir,

I have to acknowledge the receipt of your letter of the 21st instant, forwarding, for submission to His Excellency the Lord Lieutenant, the Returns of Local Taxation in Ireland for the Year 1893.

I am, Sir,

Your obedient servant,

D. HARREL.

The Secretary,

Local Government Board,

Custom House.

www.ingramcontent.com/pod-product-compliance
Lightning Source LLC
Chambersburg PA
CBHW021544270326
41930CB00008B/1356